SOME TREES

By John Ashbery

POETRY

Turandot and Other Poems
Some Trees
The Tennis Court Oath
Selected Poems
Rivers and Mountains
The Double Dream of Spring
Three Poems
Self-Portrait in a Convex Mirror
Houseboat Days

FICTION

A Nest of Ninnies (with James Schuyler)

THE AMERICAN POETRY SERIES

SOME
TREES
JOHN
ASHBERY

THE ECCO PRESS

NEW YORK

This edition issued in 1978 by The Ecco Press
1 West 30th Street, New York, N.Y. 10001
Distributed in Canada by Penguin Books Canada Limited
Printed in the United States of America

The Ecco Press logo by Ahmed Yacoubi

A few of the poems in this collection originally appeared in the
following magazines: *Folder, The Harvard Advocate, The
Kenyon Review, New World Writing, Partisan Review, Poetry,*
and *Quarterly Review of Literature.*

Library of Congress Cataloging in Publication Data

Ashbery, John.
   Some trees.
   (The American poetry series; 14)
   Originally published in 1956.
   I. Title
PS3501.S475S6   1978   811'.5'4   77-22487
ISBN 0-912-94647-4

Contents

to my parents

TWO SCENES

I

We see us as we truly behave:
From every corner comes a distinctive offering.
The train comes bearing joy;
The sparks it strikes illuminate the table.
Destiny guides the water-pilot, and it is destiny.
For long we hadn't heard so much news, such noise.
The day was warm and pleasant.
"We see you in your hair,
Air resting around the tips of mountains."

II

A fine rain anoints the canal machinery.
This is perhaps a day of general honesty
Without example in the world's history
Though the fumes are not of a singular authority
And indeed are dry as poverty.
Terrific units are on an old man
In the blue shadow of some paint cans
As laughing cadets say, "In the evening
Everything has a schedule, if you can find out what it is."

POPULAR SONGS

He continued to consult her for her beauty
(The host gone to a longing grave).
The story then resumed in day coaches
Both bravely eyed the finer dust on the blue. That summer
("The worst ever") she stayed in the car with the cur.
That was something between her legs.
Alton had been getting letters from his mother
About the payments — half the flood
Over and what about the net rest of the year?
Who cares? Anyway (you know how thirsty they were)
The extra worry began it — on the
Blue blue mountain — she never set foot
And then and there. Meanwhile the host
Mourned her quiet tenure. They all stayed chatting.
No one did much about eating.
The tears came and stopped, came and stopped, until
Becoming the guano-lightened summer night landscape,
All one glow, one mild laugh lasting ages.
Some precision, he fumed into his soup.

You laugh. There is no peace in the fountain.
The footmen smile and shift. The mountain
Rises nightly to disappointed stands
Dining in "The Gardens of the Moon."

There is no way to prevent this
Or the expectation of disappointment.
All are aware, some carry a secret
Better, of hands emulating deeds
Of days untrustworthy. But these may decide.
The face extended its sorrowing light
Far out over them. And now silent as a group
The actors prepare their first decline.

ECLOGUE

Cuddie: Slowly all your secret is had
        In the empty day. People and sticks go down to
           the water.
        How can we be so silent? Only shivers
        Are bred in this land of whistling goats.

Colin: Father, I have long dreamed your whitened
        Face and sides to accost me in dull play.
        If you in your bush indeed know her
        Where shall my heart's vagrant tides place her?

Cuddie: A wish is induced by a sudden change
        In the wind's decay. Shall we to the water's
           edge,
        O prince? The peons rant in a light fume.
        Madness will gaze at its reflection.

Colin: What is this pain come near me?
        Now I thought my heart would burst,
        And there, spiked like some cadenza's head,
        A tiny crippled heart was born.

Cuddie: I tell you good will imitate this.
Now we must dip in raw water
These few thoughts and fleshy members.
So evil may refresh our days.

Colin: She has descended part way!
Now father cut me down with tears.
Plant me far in my mother's image
To do cold work of books and stones.

Cuddie: I need not raise my hand

Colin: *She burns the flying peoples*

Cuddie: To hear its old advice

Colin: *And spears my heart's two beasts*

Cuddie: Or cover with its mauves.

Colin: *And I depart unhurt.*

THE INSTRUCTION MANUAL

As I sit looking out of a window of the building
I wish I did not have to write the instruction manual on
    the uses of a new metal.
I look down into the street and see people, each walking
    with an inner peace,
And envy them — they are so far away from me!
Not one of them has to worry about getting out this
    manual on schedule.
And, as my way is, I begin to dream, resting my elbows
    on the desk and leaning out of the window a little,
Of dim Guadalajara! City of rose-colored flowers!
City I wanted most to see, and most did not see, in Mexico!
But I fancy I see, under the press of having to write the
    instruction manual,
Your public square, city, with its elaborate little bandstand!
The band is playing *Scheherazade* by Rimsky- Korsakov.
Around stand the flower girls, handing out rose- and
    lemon-colored flowers,
Each attractive in her rose-and-blue striped dress (Oh! such
    shades of rose and blue),
And nearby is the little white booth where women in green
    serve you green and yellow fruit.
The couples are parading; everyone is in a holiday mood.

First, leading the parade, is a dapper fellow
Clothed in deep blue. On his head sits a white hat
And he wears a mustache, which has been trimmed for
    the occasion.
His dear one, his wife, is young and pretty; her shawl is
    rose, pink, and white.
Her slippers are patent leather, in the American fashion,
And she carries a fan, for she is modest, and does not want
    the crowd to see her face too often.
But everybody is so busy with his wife or loved one
I doubt they would notice the mustachioed man's wife.
Here come the boys! They are skipping and throwing
    little things on the sidewalk
Which is made of gray tile. One of them, a little older,
    has a toothpick in his teeth.
He is silenter than the rest, and affects not to notice the
    pretty young girls in white.
But his friends notice them, and shout their jeers at the
    laughing girls.
Yet soon all this will cease, with the deepening of their
    years,
And love bring each to the parade grounds for another
    reason.
But I have lost sight of the young fellow with the tooth-
    pick.
Wait — there he is — on the other side of the bandstand,

Secluded from his friends, in earnest talk with a young girl
Of fourteen or fifteen. I try to hear what they are saying
But it seems they are just mumbling something — shy
    words of love, probably.
She is slightly taller than he, and looks quietly down into
    his sincere eyes.
She is wearing white. The breeze ruffles her long fine
    black hair against her olive cheek.
Obviously she is in love. The boy, the young boy with
    the toothpick, he is in love too;
His eyes show it. Turning from this couple,
I see there is an intermission in the concert.
The paraders are resting and sipping drinks through straws
(The drinks are dispensed from a large glass crock by a
    lady in dark blue),
And the musicians mingle among them, in their creamy
    white uniforms, and talk
About the weather, perhaps, or how their kids are doing
    at school.

Let us take this opportunity to tiptoe into one of the side
    streets.
Here you may see one of those white houses with green
    trim
That are so popular here. Look — I told you!
It is cool and dim inside, but the patio is sunny.

An old woman in gray sits there, fanning herself with a
  palm leaf fan.
She welcomes us to her patio, and offers us a cooling drink.
"My son is in Mexico City," she says. "He would welcome
  you too
If he were here. But his job is with a bank there.
Look, here is a photograph of him."
And a dark-skinned lad with pearly teeth grins out at us
  from the worn leather frame.
We thank her for her hospitality, for it is getting late
And we must catch a view of the city, before we leave,
  from a good high place.
That church tower will do — the faded pink one, there
  against the fierce blue of the sky. Slowly we enter.
The caretaker, an old man dressed in brown and gray,
  asks us how long we have been in the city, and how
  we like it here.
His daughter is scrubbing the steps — she nods to us as we
  pass into the tower.
Soon we have reached the top, and the whole network of
  the city extends before us.
There is the rich quarter, with its houses of pink and
  white, and its crumbling, leafy terraces.
There is the poorer quarter, its homes a deep blue.
There is the market, where men are selling hats and
  swatting flies

And there is the public library, painted several shades of
    pale green and beige.
Look! There is the square we just came from, with the
    promenaders.
There are fewer of them, now that the heat of the day has
    increased,
But the young boy and girl still lurk in the shadows of the
    bandstand.
And there is the home of the little old lady —
She is still sitting in the patio, fanning herself.
How limited, but how complete withal, has been our
    experience of Guadalajara!
We have seen young love, married love, and the love of an
    aged mother for her son.
We have heard the music, tasted the drinks, and looked at
    colored houses.
What more is there to do, except stay? And that we can-
    not do.
And as a last breeze freshens the top of the weathered old
    tower, I turn my gaze
Back to the instruction manual which has made me dream
    of Guadalajara.

THE GRAPEVINE

Of who we and all they are
You all now know. But you know
After they began to find us out we grew
Before they died thinking us the causes

Of their acts. Now we'll not know
The truth of some still at the piano, though
They often date from us, causing
These changes we think we are. We don't care

Though, so tall up there
In young air. But things get darker as we move
To ask them: Whom must we get to know
To die, so you live and we know?

A BOY

I'll do what the raids suggest,
Dad, and that other livid window,
But the tide pushes an awful lot of monsters
And I think it's my true fate.

It had been raining but
It had not been raining.

No one could begin to mop up this particular mess.
Thunder lay down in the heart.
"My child, I love any vast electrical disturbance."
Disturbance! Could the old man, face in the rainweed,

Ask more smuttily? By night it charged over plains,
Driven from Dallas and Oregon, always *whither*,
Why not now? The boy seemed to have fallen
From shelf to shelf of someone's rage.

That night it rained on the boxcars, explaining
The thought of the pensive cabbage roses near the boxcars.
My boy. Isn't there something I asked you once?
What happened? It's also farther to the corner
Aboard the maple furniture. *He*
Couldn't lie. He'd tell 'em by their syntax.

But listen now in the flood.
They're throwing up behind the lines.
Dry fields of lightning rise to receive
The observer, the mincing flag. *An unendurable age.*

GLAZUNOVIANA

The man with the red hat
And the polar bear, is he here too?
The window giving on shade,
Is that here too?
And all the little helps,
My initials in the sky,
The hay of an arctic summer night?

The bear
Drops dead in sight of the window.
Lovely tribes have just moved to the north.
In the flickering evening the martins grow denser.
Rivers of wings surround us and vast tribulation.

THE HERO

Whose face is this
So stiff against the blue trees,

Lifted to the future
Because there is no end?

But that has faded
Like flowers, like the first days

Of good conduct. Visit
The strong man. Pinch him —

There is no end to his
Dislike, the accurate one.

POEM

While we were walking under the top
The road so strangely lit by lamps
And I wanting only peace
From the tradesmen who tried cutting my hair
Under their lips a white word is waiting
Hanging from a cliff like the sky

It is because of the sky
We ever reached the top
On that day of waiting
For the hand and the lamps
I moisten my crystal hair
Never so calmly as when at peace

With the broken sky of peace
Peace means it to the sky
Let down your hair
Through peaceful air the top
Of ruins because what are lamps
When night is waiting

A roomful of people waiting
To die in peace
Then strike the procession of lamps

They brought more than sky
Lungs back to the top
Means to doom your hair

Those bright pads of hair
Before the sea held back waiting
And you cannot speak to the top
It moves toward peace
And know the day of sky
Only by falling lamps

Beyond the desert lamps
Mount enslaved crystal mountains of hair
Into the day of sky
Silence is waiting
For anything peace
And you find the top

The top is lamps
Peace to the fragrant hair
Waiting for a tropical sky

ALBUM LEAF

The other marigolds and the cloths
Are crimes invented for history.
What can we achieve, aspiring?
And what, aspiring, can we achieve?

What can the rain that fell
All day on the grounds
And on the bingo tables?
Even though it is clearing,

The statue turned to a sweeter light,
The nearest patrons are black.
Then there is a storm of receipts: night,
Sand the bowl did not let fall.

The other marigolds are scattered like dust.
Sweet peas in dark gardens
Squirt false melancholy over history.
If a bug fell from so high, would it land?

THE PICTURE OF LITTLE J. A. IN A
PROSPECT OF FLOWERS

He was spoilt from childhood
by the future, which he mastered
rather early and apparently
without great difficulty.

BORIS PASTERNAK

I

Darkness falls like a wet sponge
And Dick gives Genevieve a swift punch
In the pajamas. "Aroint thee, witch."
Her tongue from previous ecstasy
Releases thoughts like little hats.

"He clap'd me first during the eclipse.
Afterwards I noted his manner
Much altered. But he sending
At that time certain handsome jewels
I durst not seem to take offence."

In a far recess of summer
Monks are playing soccer.

II

So far is goodness a mere memory
Or naming of recent scenes of badness
That even these lives, children,
You may pass through to be blessed,
So fair does each invent his virtue.

And coming from a white world, music
Will sparkle at the lips of many who are
Beloved. Then these, as dirty handmaidens
To some transparent witch, will dream
Of a white hero's subtle wooing,
And time shall force a gift on each.

That beggar to whom you gave no cent
Striped the night with his strange descant.

III

Yet I cannot escape the picture
Of my small self in that bank of flowers:
My head among the blazing phlox
Seemed a pale and gigantic fungus.
I had a hard stare, accepting

Everything, taking nothing,
As though the rolled-up future might stink
As loud as stood the sick moment
The shutter clicked. Though I was wrong,
Still, as the loveliest feelings

Must soon find words, and these, yes,
Displace them, so I am not wrong
In calling this comic version of myself
The true one. For as change is horror,
Virtue is really stubbornness

And only in the light of lost words
Can we imagine our rewards.

PANTOUM

Eyes shining without mystery,
Footprints eager for the past
Through the vague snow of many clay pipes,
And what is in store?

Footprints eager for the past,
The usual obtuse blanket.
And what is in store
For those dearest to the king?

The usual obtuse blanket?
Of legless regrets and amplifications
For those dearest to the king.
Yes, sirs, connoisseurs of oblivion,

Of legless regrets and amplifications,
That is why a watchdog is shy.
Yes, sirs, connoisseurs of oblivion,
These days are short, brittle; there is only one night.

That is why a watchdog is shy,
Why the court, trapped in a silver storm, is dying.
These days are short, brittle; there is only one night
And that soon gotten over.

Why, the court, trapped in a silver storm, is dying!
Some blunt pretense to safety we have
And that soon gotten over
For they must have motion.

Some blunt pretense to safety we have:
Eyes shining without mystery
For they must have motion
Through the vague snow of many clay pipes.

GRAND ABACUS

Perhaps this valley too leads into the head of long-ago
    days.
What, if not its commercial and etiolated visage, could
    break through the meadow wires?
It placed a chair in the meadow and then went far away.
People come to visit in summer, they do not think about
    the head.
Soldiers come down to see the head. The stick hides from
    them.
The heavens say, "Here I am, boys and girls!"
The stick tries to hide in the noise. The leaves, happy,
    drift over the dusty meadow.
"I'd like to see it," someone said about the head, which has
    stopped pretending to be a town.
Look! A ghastly change has come over it. The ears fall
    off — they are laughing people.
The skin is perhaps children, they say, "We children,"
    and are vague near the sea. The eyes —
Wait! What large raindrops! The eyes —
Wait, can't you see them pattering, in the meadow, like
    a dog?
The eyes are all glorious! And now the river comes to
    sweep away the last of us.
Who knew it, at the beginning of the day?

It is best to travel like a comet, with the others, though one
   does not see them.
How far that bridle flashed! "Hurry up, children!" The
   birds fly back, they say, "We were lying,
We do not want to fly away." But it is already too late.
   The children have vanished.

THE MYTHOLOGICAL POET

I

The music brought us what it seemed
We had long desired, but in a form
So rarefied there was no emptiness
Of sensation, as if pleasure
Might persist, like a dear friend
Walking toward one in a dream.
It was the toothless murmuring
Of ancient willows, who kept their trouble
In a stage of music. Without tumult
Snow-capped mountains and heart-shaped
Cathedral windows were contained
There, until only infinity
Remained of beauty. Then lighter than the air
We rose and packed the picnic basket.

But there is beside us, they said,
Whom we do not sustain, the world
Of things, that rages like a virgin
Next to our silken thoughts. It can
Be touched, they said. It cannot harm.

But suddenly their green sides
Foundered, as if the virgin beat
Their airy trellis from within.

Over her furious sighs, a new
Music, innocent and monstrous
As the ocean's bright display of teeth
Fell on the jousting willows. We
Are sick, they said. It is a warning
We were not meant to understand.

II

The mythological poet, his face
Fabulous and fastidious, accepts
Beauty before it arrives. The heavenly
Moment in the heaviness of arrival
Deplores him. He is merely
An ornament, a kind of lewd
Cloud placed on the horizon.

Close to the zoo, acquiescing
To dust, candy, perverts; inserted in
The panting forest, or openly
Walking in the great and sullen square
He has eloped with all music
And does not care. For isn't there,
He says, a final diversion, greater
Because it can be given, a gift
Too simple even to be despised?

And oh beside the roaring
Centurion of the lion's hunger
Might not child and pervert
Join hands, in the instant
Of their interest, in the shadow
Of a million boats; their hunger
From loss grown merely a gesture?

SONNET

Each servant stamps the reader with a look.
After many years he has been brought nothing.
The servant's frown is the reader's patience.
The servant goes to bed.
The patience rambles on
Musing on the library's lofty holes.

His pain is the servant's alive.
It pushes to the top stain of the wall
Its tree-top's head of excitement:
Baskets, birds, beetles, spools.
The light walls collapse next day.
Traffic is the reader's pictured face.
Dear, be the tree your sleep awaits;
Worms be your words, you not safe from ours.

CHAOS

Don't ask me to go there again
The white is too painful
Better to forget it
the sleeping river spoke to the awake land

When they first drew the wires
across the field
slowly air settled
on the pools
The blue mirror came to light
Then someone feared the pools
To be armor enough might not someone
draw down the sky
Light emerged
The swimming motion

At last twilight that will not protect the leaves
Death that will not try to scream
Black beaches
That is why I sent you the black postcard that will never
    deafen

That is why land urges the well
The white is running in its grooves
The river slides under our dreams
but land flows more silently

THE ORIOLES

What time the orioles came flying
Back to the homes, over the silvery dikes and seas,
The sad spring melted at a leap,
The shining clouds came over the hills to meet them.

The old house guards its memories, the birds
Stream over colored snow in summer
Or back into the magic rising sun in winter.
They cluster at the feeding station, and rags of song

Greet the neighbors. "Was that your voice?"
And in spring the mad caroling continues long after day-
    light
As each builds his hanging nest
Of pliant twigs and the softest moss and grasses.

But one morning you get up and the vermilion-colored
Messenger is there, bigger than life at the window.
"I take my leave of you; now I fly away
To the sunny reeds and marshes of my winter home."

And that night you gaze moodily
At the moonlit apple-blossoms, for of course
Horror and repulsion do exist! They do! And you wonder,

How long will the perfumed dung, the sunlit clouds
    cover my heart?

And then some morning when the snow is flying
Or it lines the black fir-trees, the light cries,
The excited songs start up in the yard!
The feeding station is glad to receive its guests,

But how long can the stopover last?
The cold begins when the last song retires,
And even when they fly against the trees in bright
        formation
You know the peace they brought was long overdue.

THE YOUNG SON

The screen of supreme good fortune curved his absolute smile into a celestial scream. These things (the most arbitrary that could exist) wakened denials, thoughts of putrid reversals as he traced the green paths to and fro. Here and there a bird sang, a rose silenced her expression of him, and all the gaga flowers wondered. But they puzzled the wanderer with their vague wearinesses. Is the conclusion, he asked, the road forced by concubines from exact meters of strategy? Surely the trees are hinged to no definite purpose or surface. Yet now a wonder would shoot up, all one color, and virtues would jostle each other to get a view of nothing — the crowded house, two faces glued fast to the mirror, corners and the bustling forest ever preparing, ever menacing its own shape with a shadow of the evil defenses gotten up and in fact already exhausted in some void of darkness, some kingdom he knew the earth could not even bother to avoid if the minutes arranged and divine lettermen with smiling cries were to come in the evening of administration and night which no cure, no bird ever more compulsory, no subject apparently intent on its heart's own demon would forestall even if the truths she told of were now being seriously lit, one by one, in the hushed and fast darkening room.

THE THINNEST SHADOW

He is sherrier
And sherriest.
A tall thermometer
Reflects him best.

Children in the street
Watch him go by.
"Is that the thinnest shadow?"
They to one another cry.

A face looks from the mirror
As if to say,
"Be supple, young man,
Since you can't be gay."

All his friends have gone
From the street corner cold.
His heart is full of lies
And his eyes are full of mold.

CANZONE

Until the first chill
No door sat on the clay.
When Billy brought on the chill
He began to chill.
No hand can
Point to the chill
It brought. Where a chill
Was, the grass grows.
See how it grows.
Acts punish the chill
Showing summer in the grass.
The acts are grass.

Acts of our grass
Transporting chill
Over brazen grass
That retorts as grass
Leave the clay,
The grass,
And that which is grass.
The far formal forest can,
Used doubts can
Sit on the grass.
Hark! The sadness grows
In pain. The shadow grows.

All that grows
In deep shadow or grass
Is lifted to what grows.
Walking, a space grows.
Beyond, weeds chill
Toward night which grows.
Looking about, nothing grows.
Now a whiff of clay
Respecting clay
Or that which grows
Brings on what can.
And no one can.

The sprinkling can
Slumbered on the dock. Clay
Leaked from a can.
Normal heads can
Touch barbed-wire grass
If they can
Sing the old song of can
Waiting for a chill
In the chill
That without a can
Is painting less clay
Therapeutic colors of clay.

We got out into the clay
As a boy can.
Yet there's another kind of clay
Not arguing clay,
As time grows
Not getting larger, but mad clay
Looked for for clay,
And grass
Begun seeming, grass
Struggling up out of clay
Into the first chill
To be quiet and raucous in the chill.

The chill
Flows over burning grass.
Not time grows.
So odd lights can
Fall on sinking clay.

ERRORS

Jealousy. Whispered weather reports.
In the street we found boxes
Littered with snow, to burn at home.
What flower tolling on the waters
You stupefied me. We waxed,
Carnivores, late and alight
In the beaded winter. All was ominous, luminous.
Beyond the bed's veils the white walls danced
Some violent compunction. Promises,
We thought then of your dry portals,
Bright cornices of eavesdropping palaces,
You were painfully stitched to hours
The moon now tears up, scoffing at the unrinsed portions.
And loves adopted realm. Flees to water,
The coach dissolving in mists.
                                        A wish
Refines the lines around the mouth
At these ten-year intervals. It fumed
Clear air of wars. It desired
Excess of core in all things. From all things sucked
A glossy denial. But look, pale day:
We fly hence. To return if sketched
In the prophet's silence. Who doubts it is true?

ILLUSTRATION

I

A novice was sitting on a cornice
High over the city. Angels

Combined their prayers with those
Of the police, begging her to come off it.

One lady promised to be her friend.
"I do not want a friend," she said.

A mother offered her some nylons
Stripped from her very legs. Others brought

Little offerings of fruit and candy,
The blind man all his flowers. If any

Could be called successful, these were,
For that the scene should be a ceremony

Was what she wanted. "I desire
Monuments," she said. "I want to move

Figuratively, as waves caress
The thoughtless shore. You people I know

48

Will offer me every good thing
I do not want. But please remember

I died accepting them." With that, the wind
Unpinned her bulky robes, and naked

As a roc's egg, she drifted softly downward
Out of the angels' tenderness and the minds of men.

II

Much that is beautiful must be discarded
So that we may resemble a taller

Impression of ourselves. Moths climb in the flame,
Alas, that wish only to be the flame:

They do not lessen our stature.
We twinkle under the weight

Of indiscretions. But how could we tell
That of the truth we know, she was

The somber vestment? For that night, rockets sighed
Elegantly over the city, and there was feasting:

There is so much in that moment!
So many attitudes toward that flame,

We might have soared from earth, watching her glide
Aloft, in her peplum of bright leaves.

But she, of course, was only an effigy
Of indifference, a miracle

Not meant for us, as the leaves are not
Winter's because it is the end.

SOME TREES

These are amazing: each
Joining a neighbor, as though speech
Were a still performance.
Arranging by chance

To meet as far this morning
From the world as agreeing
With it, you and I
Are suddenly what the trees try

To tell us we are:
That their merely being there
Means something; that soon
We may touch, love, explain.

And glad not to have invented
Such comeliness, we are surrounded:
A silence already filled with noises,
A canvas on which emerges

A chorus of smiles, a winter morning.
Placed in a puzzling light, and moving,
Our days put on such reticence
These accents seem their own defense.

HOTEL DAUPHIN

It was not something identical with my carnation-world
But its smallest possession—a hair or a sneeze—
I wanted. I remember
Dreaming on tan plush the wrong dreams

Of asking fortunes, now lost
In what snows? Is there anything
We dare credit? And we get along.
The soul resumes its teachings. Winter boats

Are visible in the harbor. A child writes
"La pluie." All noise is engendered
As we sit listening. I lose myself
In others' dreams.

Why no vacation from these fortunes, from the white hair
Of the old? These dreams of tennis?
Fortunately, the snow, cutting like a knife,
Protects too itself from us.

Not so with this rouge I send to you
At old Christmas. Here the mysteries
And the color of holly are embezzled —
Poor form, poor watchman for my holidays,

My days of name-calling and blood-letting.
Do not fear the exasperation of death
(Whichever way I go is solitary)
Or the candles blown out by your passing.

It breathes a proper farewell, the panic
Under sleep like grave under stone,
Warning of sad renewals of the spirit.
In cheap gardens, fortunes. Or we might never depart.

THE PAINTER

Sitting between the sea and the buildings
He enjoyed painting the sea's portrait.
But just as children imagine a prayer
Is merely silence, he expected his subject
To rush up the sand, and, seizing a brush,
Plaster its own portrait on the canvas.

So there was never any paint on his canvas
Until the people who lived in the buildings
Put him to work: "Try using the brush
As a means to an end. Select, for a portrait,
Something less angry and large, and more subject
To a painter's moods, or, perhaps, to a prayer."

How could he explain to them his prayer
That nature, not art, might usurp the canvas?
He chose his wife for a new subject,
Making her vast, like ruined buildings,
As if, forgetting itself, the portrait
Had expressed itself without a brush.

Slightly encouraged, he dipped his brush
In the sea, murmuring a heartfelt prayer:
"My soul, when I paint this next portrait

Let it be you who wrecks the canvas."
The news spread like wildfire through the buildings:
He had gone back to the sea for his subject.

Imagine a painter crucified by his subject!
Too exhausted even to lift his brush,
He provoked some artists leaning from the buildings
To malicious mirth: "We haven't a prayer
Now, of putting ourselves on canvas,
Or getting the sea to sit for a portrait!"

Others declared it a self-portrait.
Finally all indications of a subject
Began to fade, leaving the canvas
Perfectly white. He put down the brush.
At once a howl, that was also a prayer,
Arose from the overcrowed buildings.

They tossed him, the portrait, from the tallest of the
        buildings;
And the sea devoured the canvas and the brush
As though his subject had decided to remain a prayer.

AND YOU KNOW

The girls, protected by gold wire from the gaze
Of the onrushing students, live in an atmosphere of
    vacuum
In the old schoolhouse covered with nasturtiums.
At night, comets, shootings stars, twirling planets,
Suns, bits of illuminated pumice, and spooks hang over
    the old place;
The atmosphere is breathless. Some find the summer light
Nauseous and damp, but there are those
Who are charmed by it, going out into the morning.
We must rest here, for this is where the teacher comes.
On his desk stands a vase of tears.
A quiet feeling pervades the playroom. His voice clears
Through the interminable afternoon: "I was a child once
Under the spangled sun. Now I do what must be done.
I teach reading and writing and flaming arithmetic. Those
In my home come to me anxiously at night, asking how
    it goes.
My door is always open. I never lie, and the great heat
    warms me."

His door is always open, the fond schoolmaster!
We ought to imitate him in our lives,
For as a man lives, he dies. To pass away

In the afternoon, on the vast vapid bank
You think is coming to crown you with hollyhocks and
    lilacs, or in gold at the opera,
Requires that one shall have lived so much! And not
    merely
Asking questions and giving answers, but grandly sitting,
Like a great rock, through many years.
It is the erratic path of time we trace
On the globe, with moist fingertip, and surely, the globe
    stops;
We are pointing to England, to Africa, to Nigeria;
And we shall visit these places, you and I, and other
    places,
Including heavenly Naples, queen of the sea, where I shall
    be king and you will be queen,
And all the places around Naples.
So the good old teacher is right, to stop with his finger on
    Naples, gazing out into the mild December afternoon
As his star pupil enters the classroom in that elaborate
    black and yellow creation.
He is thinking of her flounces, and is caught in them as if
    they were made of iron, they will crush him to
    death!
Goodbye, old teacher, we must travel on, not to a better
    land, perhaps,
But to the England of the sonnets, Paris, Colombia, and
    Switzerland

And all the places with names, that we wish to visit —
Strasbourg, Albania,
The coast of Holland, Madrid, Singapore, Naples, Salonika,
    Liberia, and Turkey.
So we leave you behind with her of the black and yellow
    flounces.
You were always a good friend, but a special one.
Now as we brush through the clinging leaves we seem to
    hear you crying;
You want us to come back, but it is too late to come back,
    isn't it?
It is too late to go to the places with the names (what were
    they, anyway? just names).
It is too late to go anywhere but to the nearest star, that
    one, that hangs just over the hill, beckoning
Like a hand of which the arm is not visible. Goodbye,
    Father! Goodbye, pupils. Goodbye, my master and
    my dame.
We fly to the nearest star, whether it be red like a furnace,
    or yellow,
And we carry your lessons in our hearts (the lessons and
    our hearts are the same)
Out of the humid classroom, into the forever. Goodbye,
    Old Dog Tray.

And so they have left us feeling tired and old.
They never cared for school anyway.

And they have left us with the things pinned on the
   bulletin board,
And the night, the endless, muggy night that is invading
   our school.

HE

He cuts down the lakes so they appear straight
He smiles at his feet in their tired mules.
He turns up the music much louder.
He takes down the vaseline from the pantry shelf.

He is the capricious smile behind the colored bottles.
He eats not lest the poor want some.
He breathes of attitudes the piney altitudes.
He indeed is the White Cliffs of Dover.

He knows that his neck is frozen.
He snorts in the vale of dim wolves.
He writes to say, "If ever you visit this island,
He'll grow you back to your childhood.

"He is the liar behind the hedge
He grew one morning out of candor.
He is his own consolation prize.
He has had his eye on you from the beginning."

He hears the weak cut down with a smile.
He waltzes tragically on the spitting housetops.
He is never near. What you need
He cancels with the air of one making a salad.

He is always the last to know.
He is strength you once said was your bonnet.
He has appeared in "Carmen."
He is after us. If you decide

He is important, it will get you nowhere.
He is the source of much bitter reflection.
He used to be pretty for a rat.
He is now over-proud of his Etruscan appearance.

He walks in his sleep into your life.
He is worth knowing only for the children
He has reared as savages in Utah.
He helps his mother take in the clothes-line.

He is unforgettable as a shooting star.
He is known as "Liverlips."
He will tell you he has had a bad time of it.
He will try to pretend his pressagent is a temptress.

He looks terrible on the stairs.
He cuts himself on what he eats.
He was last seen flying to New York.
He was handing out cards which read:

"He wears a question in his left eye.
He dislikes the police but will associate with them.

He will demand something not on the menu.
He is invisible to the eyes of beauty and culture.

"He prevented the murder of Mistinguett in Mexico.
He has a knack for abortions. If you see
He is following you, forget him immediately:
He is dangerous even though asleep and unarmed."

MEDITATIONS OF A PARROT

Oh the rocks and the thimble
The oasis and the bed
Oh the jacket and the roses.

All sweetly stood up the sea to me
Like blue cornflakes in a white bowl.
The girl said, "Watch this."

I come from Spain, I said.
I was purchased at a fair.
She said, "None of us know.

"There was a house once
Of dazzling canopies
And halls like a keyboard.

"These the waves tore in pieces."
(His old wound —
And all day! Robin Hood! Robin Hood!)

A LONG NOVEL

What will his crimes become, now that her hands
Have gone to sleep? He gathers deeds

In the pure air, the agent
Of their factual excesses. He laughs as she inhales.

If it could have ended before
It began — the sorrow, the snow

Dropping, dropping its fine regrets.
The myrtle dries about his lavish brow.

He stands quieter than the day, a breath
In which all evils are one.

He is the purest air. But her patience,
The imperative Become, trembles

Where hands have been before. In the foul air
Each snowflake seems a Piranesi

Dropping in the past; his words are heavy
With their final meaning. Milady! Mimosa! So the end

Was the same: the discharge of spittle

Into frozen air. Except that, in a new

Humorous landscape, without music,
Written by music, he knew he was a saint,

While she touched all goodness
As golden hair, knowing its goodness

Impossible, and waking and waking
As it grew in the eyes of the beloved.

THE WAY THEY TOOK

The green bars on you grew soberer
As I petted the lock, a crank
In my specially built shoes.
We hedged about leisure, feeling, walking
That day, that night. The day
Came up. The heads borne in peach vessels
Out of asking that afternoon droned.
You saw the look of some other people,
Huge husks of chattering boys
And girls unfathomable in lovely dresses
And remorseful and on the edge of darkness.
No firmness in that safe smile ebbing.
Tinkling sadness. The sun pissed on a rock.

That is how I came nearer
To what was on my shoulder. One day you were lunch-
  ing
With a friend's mother; I thought how plebeian all this
  testimony,
That you might care to crave that, somehow
Before I would decide. Just think,
But I know now how romantic, how they whispered
Behind the lace of their aspiring
Opinions. And heaven will not care,

To raise our love
In scathing hymns. So beware and
Bye now. The jewels are for luck.

SONNET

The barber at his chair
Clips me. He does as he goes.
He clips the hairs outside the nose.
Too many preparations, nose!
I see the raincoat this Saturday.
A building is against the sky —
The result is more sky.
Something gathers in painfully.

To be the razor — how would you like to be
The razor, blue with ire,
That presses me? This is the wrong way.
The canoe speeds toward a waterfall.
Something, prince, in our backward manners —
You guessed the reason for the storm.

THE PIED PIPER

Under the day's crust a half-eaten child
And further sores which eyesight shall reveal
And they live. But what of dark elders
Whose touch at nightfall must now be
To keep their promise? Misery
Starches the host's one bed, his hand
Falls like an axe on her curls:
"Come in, come in! Better that the winter
Blaze unseen, than we two sleep apart!"

Who in old age will often part
From single sleep at the murmur
Of acerb revels under the hill;
Whose children couple as the earth crumbles
In vanity forever going down
A sunlit road, for his love was strongest
Who never loved them at all, and his notes
Most civil, laughing not to return.

ANSWERING A QUESTION IN THE MOUNTAINS

I

I went into the mountains to interest myself
In the fabulous dinners of hosts distant and demure.

The foxes followed with endless lights.

Some day I am to build the wall
Of the box in which all angles are shown.
I shall bounce like a ball.
The towers of justice are waving
To describe the angles we describe.
Oh we have been so far
To instruct the birds in our cold ways.

Near me I heard a sound,
The line of a match struck in care.

It is late to be late.

II

Let us ascend the hearts in our hearts.
Let us ascend trees in our heads,
The dull heads of trees.

It is pain in the hand of the ungodly
To witness all the sentries,
The perfumed toque of dawn,
The hysteric evening with empty hands.
The snow creeps by; many light years pass.

We see for the first time.
We shall see for the first time.
We have seen for the first time.

The snow creeps by; many light years pass.

III

I cannot agree or seek
Since I departed in the laugh of diamonds
The hosts of my young days.

A PASTORAL

Perhaps no vice endears me to the showboat,
Whose license permeates our deep south.
The shows are simple, not yet easy, with handsome
And toy horns trying tried and true melodies.
Silently, that vice might speak from the shade:
"Your capers have misdirected all your animals."

But, hating and laughing, risen with animals,
Who is denied admission to the showboat?
Nevertheless, because of tomorrow's shade
The lad intends to file with the green deep south.
His ankles seek the temple melodies.
His mischief stirs the rocks and keeps them handsome.

Tomorrow, finding them less handsome,
They might side with the foreseeing of animals.
From the corral the melodies
Would start, teaching the showboat
(Thick is the tambour, oversold the deep south)
Which flowers to press back into the shade.

My affairs wrapped in shade,
Myself shall mobilize that handsome
Energetic enemy of the deep south.

Lately worms have pestered the animals.
Alarmed at our actions, a glittering showboat
Fled from the glade of supposed melodies.

And no more in our society living melodies
Break forth under the little or no shade.
The days are guarded. A miserable showboat
Plies back and forth between the handsome
Rocks, unwatched by animals
Whose glistening breath wakens forgetfulness of the deep
    south.

Truly the lesson of the deep south
Is how to avoid lingering beyond melodies
That cleave to the heart before it learns the animals
Strangers are. Knowing shade
Is their apology, let us never excuse handsome
Terror, the crook'd finger of a disappearing showboat.

The psalmist thought the deep south a wonderful showboat
And to the animals he met in the shade
Said, "You are my melodies, and you are handsome."

LE LIVRE EST SUR LA TABLE

I

All beauty, resonance, integrity,
Exist by deprivation or logic
Of strange position. This being so,

We can only imagine a world in which a woman
Walks and wears her hair and knows
All that she does not know. Yet we know

What her breasts are. And we give fullness
To the dream. The table supports the book,
The plume leaps in the hand. But what

Dismal scene is this? the old man pouting
At a black cloud, the woman gone
Into the house, from which the wailing starts?

II

The young man places a bird-house
Against the blue sea. He walks away
And it remains. Now other

Men appear, but they live in boxes.
The sea protects them like a wall.
The gods worship a line-drawing

Of a woman, in the shadow of the sea
Which goes on writing. Are there
Collisions, communications on the shore

Or did all secrets vanish when
The woman left? Is the bird mentioned
In the waves' minutes, or did the land advance?

John Ashbery was born in Rochester in 1927, grew up on a farm in western New York State, and received his education at Deerfield Academy, Harvard University, and Columbia University. From 1955 to 1965 he lived and worked in France, during which time three books of his poems were published in the United States. From 1965 to 1972 he was Executive Editor of *ARTnews*, and he is teaching at present in the Creative Writing Program at Brooklyn College.

Mr. Ashbery's most recent books of poems include *Houseboat Days* (1977), *Rivers and Mountains* (new Ecco Press edition, 1977), *The Double Dream of Spring* (new Ecco Press edition, 1976), and *Self-Portrait in a Convex Mirror* (1975). He is also the author of three plays and numerous critical essays and translations, and is co-author with James Schuyler of a novel, *A Nest of Ninnies*. In 1976, John Ashbery received the Pulitzer Prize, the National Book Award, and the National Book Critics Circle Award for his poetry.